SCHIRMER PERFORMANCE EDITIONS

J.S. BACH
SELECTIONS FROM THE NOTEBOOK FOR ANNA MAGDALENA BACH

Edited and Recorded by Christos Tsitsaros

To access companion recorded performances online, visit:
www.halleonard.com/mylibrary

Enter Code
7129-0987-6756-1035

On the cover:
A Young Lady Seated at a Virginal c.1670
by Jan Vermeer
(1632-1675)

©Bridgeman Art Library, Getty Images

ISBN-13: 978-0-634-09905-2
ISBN-10: 0-634-09905-1

G. SCHIRMER, Inc.

DISTRIBUTED BY

HAL•LEONARD®
CORPORATION
7777 W. BLUEMOUND RD. P.O. BOX 13819 MILWAUKEE, WI 53213

www.musicsalesclassical.com
www.halleonard.com

CONTENTS

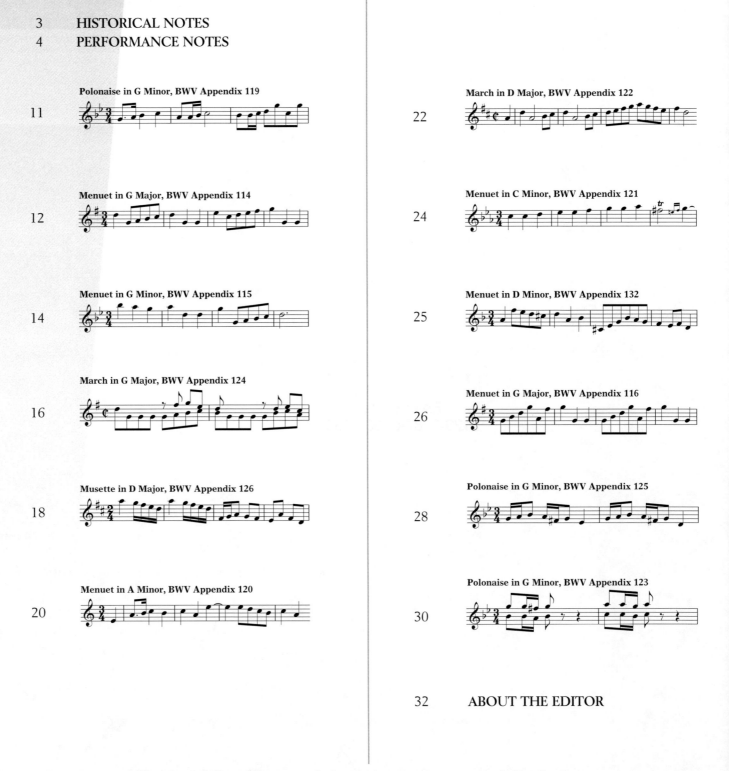

The price of this publication includes access to companion recorded performances online, for download or streaming, using the unique code found on the title page.
Visit **www.halleonard.com/mylibrary** and enter the access code.

HISTORICAL NOTES

THE MOST FAMOUS KEYBOARD NOTEBOOK

When Johann Sebastian Bach (1685-1750) married his second wife in 1721, he was already an established organist, court and chamber musician, and Kapellmeister. His new bride, the twenty-year-old Anna Magdalena Wilcke, came from a prestigious family of musicians and was herself an accomplished singer. In fact, she was employed at the Cöthen court, where her husband served as court conductor. After their marriage, the couple started right away on a keyboard notebook (*Clavier-Büchlein* in German) for Anna Magdalena's practice. Eventually they collected two separate books (begun in 1722 and 1725), which are known today as the *Notebook for Anna Magdalena Bach*. Anna Magdalena's musicianship and work ethic proved to be a valuable asset to the family; for, in addition to being Bach's principal copyist, she also provided opportunities, in part through her Keyboard Notebook, for the whole family to make music together.

To a music student 300 years ago, a keyboard notebook occupied a central place in one's music library. Such a notebook held works by a number of composers, including one's own teacher. The pieces demonstrated stylistic variety in the form of dance suites, preludes, fugues, and chorales. Due to the high cost of printed music, the student would transcribe most of the pieces in the notebook by hand. Students would also write their own compositions in their keyboard notebooks, since composition formed a critical part of their music training. For the most part, these books were intended for use in the home, not as professional publications.

J.S. Bach likely had his own keyboard notebook as a child, but it evidently has not survived. At a fairly early age, however, he coveted his brother's notebook, which Christoph had painstakingly collected when he was a pupil of Pachelbel (a composer known today largely for his *Canon in D*). Christoph's book included several pieces by his famous teacher, but after Johann Sebastian had copied it—which he did by hand and in complete secrecy—his brother immediately confiscated it.

Anna Magdalena's notebooks occupied a perfectly ordinary place in her musical life, but the contents make them extraordinary. The five short harpsichord suites that open the set eventually became Bach's *French Suites*, so named for the collection of short, stylized dance forms that originated in France. In addition to other pieces written by Bach, the notebooks include works by Couperin, Stolzel, Petzold, and Hasse. Anna Magdalena's talent as a singer is evident in the numerous songs and arias, including the "Aria" from the *Goldberg Variations*, purportedly her favorite composition by her husband. The pieces were hand-written by Johann Sebastian, Anna Magdalena, or one of their sons, but several of whom became successful composers. A number of the pieces have no author attributed to them, but scholars believe that Anna Magdalena or one of the children wrote many of them.

The notebooks undoubtedly occupied a central place in the Bach family's musical life, and Anna Magdalena was probably quite proud of them. She even created a decorative front cover for her collection. She gathered the music over the course of fifteen years, and, although scholars estimate that the original notebook held as many as 75 pages, sadly only 25 remain today. We can only imagine what is missing from history's most important keyboard notebook.

—Denise Pilmer Taylor

PERFORMANCE NOTES

This edition contains selected short dances from the second of the two notebooks that comprise the *Notebook for Anna Magdalena Bach*. These include the Menuets and Polonaises, the Musette in D Major, and the two Marches in G and D Major. All are short *galant* pieces in the French high-Baroque style, characterized by a light, often two-voiced texture and vocally-inspired melodies. Most of the dances are in binary form, with each of the two sections repeated.

Style and Interpretation

Several stylistic considerations led me to the editorial choices in this edition, as well as to the interpretation of the pieces in the accompanying CD. Most important was the character of each dance as expressed by a combination of musical elements including tempo, articulation, and dynamics. I have found Carl Philipp Emanuel Bach's *Essay on the True Art of Playing Keyboard Instruments* to be the most reliable and illuminating guide to the appropriate interpretation and performance of the French *galant* style so prevalent in these dances. This, not only because it contains a very detailed account of specific, eighteenth-century instrumental performance practices, but because C.P.E. Bach, like Anna Magdalena, was very fond of the French *galant* style.

In his chapter on performance, in particular, C.P.E. Bach cites "The ability through singing or playing to make the ear conscious of the true *'affect'* [character, or sentiment] of a composition," as the primary characteristic of a good performance. According to him, two prerequisites for such a clear and expressive performance are the correct timing and volume with which all notes and embellishments are to be produced. In the same chapter, he establishes connections between tempo and articulation, and indicates an indispensable way of promoting a true musical understanding of the character of the piece—listening to other soloists and ensembles.

In keeping with 18th-century performance practices, I have varied the repeats in each piece in the recording that accompanies this edition. Some principles of variation I followed include:

- The use of different dynamics or articulation in the repeated section.

- The addition of new, or the modification of existing ornaments.

- The use of a melodic variation containing passing tones, modified rhythmic figures or intervals, as well as harmonized cadences.

Naturally, students are not obliged to vary the repeats. However, if they choose to do so, I would strongly encourage them to invent or improvise their own variations.

Tempo and Articulation

The tempos adopted in the recording are based on my personal taste and musical concept. I invite students and teachers to experiment with a variety of different tempos and moods. The same is true for the articulation, phrasing, and dynamics. One of the more rewarding aspects of studying these exquisite miniatures is the discovery of the expressive possibilities they offer, the wide gamut of emotion they convey, and the evocative power and timeless humanity they encompass.

One way students can better understand the *"affect"* of each piece, as well as the most appropriate means of expression in performance, is by considering the type of dance represented by the piece, and the relationship between its time signature and rhythmic values.

In his book *Keyboard Interpretation from the 14th to the 19th Century*, Howard Ferguson mentions that the most important point in determining tempo is the prevailing texture and harmonic movement of a piece:

> "A piece that is full of demi-semiquavers [sixteenth notes] or very complicated ornamentation, or one that has harmonic shifts on every quaver [eighth note], is likely to require a comparatively slow crochet [quarter note]; while a piece that has no note smaller than quaver [eighth], little ornamentation, and a change of harmony only once every minim [half note], will need a crochet [quarter] that is comparatively quick."

In choosing appropriate articulation for the dances in this edition, one may look to the character as well as the tempo of each dance as a guide. In the opening two-measure motive of the Menuet in G Major, BWV Appendix 116, for example, the string-like character of the first half of the motive suggests *legato* eighth notes, whereas the leaping gesture of the second half implies a *staccato* touch on the last two repeated G's.

Menuet in G Major, BWV Appendix 116, mm. 1-2

These leaping gestures are found again in the opening phrases in the Menuet in G Minor, BWV Appendix 115 and G Major, BWV Appendix 114.

Further examples of the importance of relating character and rhythmic values when choosing tempos and articulation are found in the March in G Major, BWV Appendix 124, and the March in D Major, BWV Appendix 122. Both are in cut time, and, with few exceptions, the shortest rhythmic value is an eighth note. These facts suggest that the tempo in both pieces should be quite fast. The quick pace, coupled with the brilliant and spirited character of each piece, implies more detached, *non-legato* articulations, as indicated in the excerpts below.

March in G Major, BWV Appendix 124, mm. 1-2

March in D Major, BWV Appendix 122, mm. 1-2

As C.P.E. Bach states, "In general, the briskness of *allegros* is expressed by detached notes and the tenderness of *adagios* by broad, slurred notes." But he also adds, "I use the word, 'in general,' advisedly, for I am well aware that all kinds of execution may appear in any tempo." This clarification is particularly significant for teachers and performers who might otherwise feel compelled to adopt a more rigid stance to articulation based on a given rule or convention.

In general, both musically and technically, a *staccato* touch is appropriate for longer note values, such as eighth notes. Take, for example, the opening measures of the Musette in D Major, BWV Appendix 126. The broken octaves in the left-hand accompaniment suggest a *staccato* touch, which is musically effective and also technically helpful, preventing the hand from tensing while playing the broken octaves over a prolonged period (especially for younger players). The right-hand 16th-note patterns would be played *legato*, with an energetic impulse to produce the desired brilliance.

Musette in D Major, BWV Appendix 126, mm. 1-4

The eighth notes in mm. 13-16 of the Musette may be played in a variety of ways, all equally justifiable, depending upon the desired musical or harmonic effect. The examples below illustrate several possible choices.

Musette in D Major, BWV Appendix 126, mm. 13-16

Questions concerning articulation and phrasing become vastly more problematic when we apply some of the 18th-century rules and conventions to performances on modern instruments with heavier actions. In the recording of the Polonaise in G Minor, BWV Appendix 119, for example, I have included two different versions: one, a more *legato* performance befitting a modern instrument, and another more percussive performance in the detached manner reminiscent of a harpsichord. Although both interpretations are valid for different reasons, it would be more realistic to expect a less-experienced piano student to play this Polonaise in the *legato* manner, for that interpretation makes fewer demands on a student's technical skills.

Phrasing and Dynamics

In the hands of a knowledgeable teacher, the absence of dynamics and slurs in the music of Bach and his contemporaries may serve as a springboard for students to develop the skill of making well-informed choices regarding phrase structure, form, and melodic and harmonic analysis. By interrelating those aspects with tempo, articulation, and character, the student will gain the experience necessary to handle similar and more advanced pieces from the same style period.

Several general considerations about the music will influence dynamic choices. Some are listed here as a guide:

Direction of the Melodic Line
Often, one can enliven the shape of ascending melodic patterns with an even and subtle *crescendo*, and descending ones with a *diminuendo*. This, however, is by no means a general rule, and one should be cautioned against exaggerated nuances.

Dissonances
All dissonances, such as *appoggiaturas* and accented non-harmonic tones, should be stressed.

Phrase Structure
In many cases, short sub-phrases can be distinguished by varying dynamic levels slightly—for example, using an echo effect when a short motive is repeated. In other instances, a larger phrase can be built by the application of a broader and more continuous dynamic arc over an entire period.

Form and Underlying Harmonic Plan
The binary dance form, with its characteristic

$$\| : \text{I} \longrightarrow \text{V} : \| : \text{V} \longrightarrow \text{I} : \|$$

harmonic structure, provides excellent opportunities for dynamic variation. Part or all of each repeat can be executed with different dynamics. The performer should also consider a variety of other harmonic elements, such as stable and unstable harmonies, chromatic chords, and cadences.

In short, there is virtually no hard and fast rule in the selection of dynamics and phrasing, and the player or teacher is invited to make choices using well-informed musical intuition.

Pedal

The use of pedal in Baroque music is an area of controversy among teachers and performers. I believe that it should be left to the performer's discretion to use touches of pedal in order to highlight selected expressive points, with due care not to obscure the linear texture. For the less experienced player, however, the use of the pedal combined with the intricacies of texture and fingering in this music may be out of reach and is best postponed for a later time.

Fingering

The fingerings in the present edition are based on three main factors:

- musical content, with special emphasis on articulation and tempo;

- technical aspects;

- the estimated proficiency of students likely to be studying this repertoire.

Since these short dances are likely to be the novice or younger pianist's first encounter with Baroque music, I gave the last factor special consideration in making fingering choices throughout the book. I aimed not only to facilitate the performance of given articulations, but also to promote smooth transitions between positions, in order to create a more connected physical sensation of the larger line. However, since these pieces can also serve as satisfying literature for older and adult students, I have occasionally included parenthetical alternate fingerings that are more sophisticated, or that require a larger hand span.

Finally, teachers and students are encouraged to use fingerings that are suited to their own technical needs while facilitating the projection of their musical concepts.

Ornamentation

The realization of ornaments in the present edition is based on the "Explanation of divers signs, showing how to play certain ornaments neatly," with which J.S. Bach's *Notebook for Wilhelm Friedemann* begins, and the ensuing *applicatio*. C.P.E. Bach's *Essay on the True Art of Playing Keyboard Instruments* sheds additional light on the correct realization of ornaments and offers some possible variants. The dances in the present volume feature only some of the ornaments listed in the *applicatio*, as well as the *Schleifer* (slide), which is described in C.P.E. Bach's *Essay*.

Following is a brief description of the ornaments found in the *Notebook for Anna Magdalena Bach*.

The Trill

C.P.E. Bach mentions that "Trills enliven melodies and therefore are indispensable." The trill invariably begins on the tone above the principal note.

The Longer Trill With or Without Suffix

C.P.E. Bach mentions that "The suffix is omitted from successive trills and from trills followed by one or more short notes which are capable of replacing [the suffix notes]."

March in G Major, BWV Appendix 124, mm. 20-22

In some cases the suffix is written out in the music, leaving no doubt about its use.

Menuet in A Minor, BWV Appendix 120, mm. 21-23

"Trills on long notes are played with the suffix regardless of subsequent stepwise descent or ascent."

Menuet in A Minor, BWV Appendix 120, mm. 27-28

Half or Short Trill *(Halb- or Prall-Triller)*

This ornament, mentioned by C.P.E. Bach in the chapter titled "Embellishments" in his *Essay*, occurs on descending stepwise three-note *legato* patterns. According to Bach, "It represents in miniature an enclosed, unsuffixed trill, introduced by either an *appoggiatura* or a principal note."

As with articulation, it is necessary to be somewhat flexible with ornamentation when teaching less experienced students. C.P.E. Bach was quite sensitive to the technical limitations of a novice player, stating, "It is possible, when necessary, to omit any…ornament, even…trills, and arrange matters so that easier ornaments may be substituted for them." For example, the half or short trill can become a useful alternative to the usual execution of trills in stepwise descending passages, such as those in the following excerpts:

Menuet in G Major, BWV Appendix 114, mm. 30-32

Menuet in G Minor, BWV Appendix 115, mm. 9-10

In the recording accompanying this edition, I have chosen to play the simplified version in all places where I have suggested this alternative version.

The Mordent

C.P.E. Bach describes the mordent as "…an essential ornament which connects notes, fills them out, and makes them brilliant." In the dances selected here from the *Notebook for Anna Magdalena Bach*, we encounter only the short mordent.

The Appoggiatura

C.P.E. Bach mentions that "*Appoggiaturas* are among the most essential embellishments. They enhance the harmony as well as the melody [and they] modify chords which would be too simple without them."

Regarding the duration of *appoggiaturas*, Bach explains, "...they take from a following tone of duple length one half of its value, and [usually] two thirds from one of triple length."

March in G Major, BWV Appendix 124, mm. 12-13

Menuet in G Major, BWV Appendix 114, mm. 7-8

Very importantly, C.P.E. Bach mentions that, with regard to their execution, "...*appoggiaturas* are louder than the following tone..." an important expressive detail often overlooked by less experienced players.

The Schleifer (Slide)

Used rather rarely, the slide helps to fill in a leap and consists of two notes that are played before the principal one.

Menuet in D Minor, BWV Appendix 132, mm. 5-6

The Individual Pieces

Polonaise in G Minor, BWV Appendix 119

Majestic in character, this polonaise calls for experimentation with a variety of dynamics, articulations, and tempos. A *portato* touch on quarter notes will emphasize the rhythmic element, whereas a mixture of *staccato* and *legato* articulations for eighth and sixteenth notes will lighten the serious character of the piece somewhat. Noteworthy are the wedge *staccato* marks on the quarter notes in mm. 11 and 13, denoting a heavily accented, sharp attack.

Menuet in G Major, BWV Appendix 114

This minuet is similar in character to the Menuet in G Major, BWV 116. The first four measures can be grouped effectively into a single large phrase with a sweeping dynamic curve that leads to the high G in m. 4. This is the only minuet in the series in which the B section begins on the Tonic chord.

Menuet in G Minor, BWV Appendix 115

The quietly sad and tender character of this minuet, with its descending, stepwise melodic gestures, requires a delicate touch and skillful phrasing to shape the melodic contour. In m. 31, I opted for a simpler, three-note ornament, despite the fact that a four-note trill arguably would be stylistically more correct.

March in G Major, BWV Appendix 124

Although not explicitly indicated from the start, two voices can be traced in the right-hand part in the opening measures. In keeping with the voicing in mm. 2-3, one could envision an upward stem on the first eighth note in the opening measure. If this march were orchestrated, the repeated eighth-note G's in the lower voice could be assigned to a percussive instrument—perhaps a *tambourin*—and the upper voice to a melodic one, such as a flute or violin. Two elements appear in the left-hand part also. Rhythmic repeated eighth notes in mm. 1-2 imitate the right-hand part and expand in mm. 10-11 and 14-15. A contrasting moving line begins in m. 3 and alternates throughout with the first element. If orchestrated, these could be assigned to percussive and stringed instruments as well. Envisioning an orchestration such as this may lead students to a more vibrant interpretation of this lively piece.

Musette in D Major, BWV Appendix 126

The duple meter and the absence of ornamentation in this piece suggest a quick tempo. One can imagine the left-hand part played by the *musette*, the French bagpipe, resulting in the so-called "drone" effect. A *staccato* articulation on most eighth notes in the piece will convey the "drone" and somewhat nasal quality that would result if the piece were played by a combination of period wind instruments and a *tambourin*.

Menuet in A Minor, BWV Appendix 120

The canon-like imitations at the beginning of this minuet can be convincingly rendered by expressively accenting the *anacrusis* (upbeat) at the beginning of each sub-phrase (for example, beat 3, m. 2).

I have recorded this minuet twice to illustrate the use of both measured and unmeasured trills in mm. 21, 23, and 27. For the left-hand trills in mm. 22 and 24, I used a simplified trill similar to that mentioned earlier. This five-note trill undoubtedly will prove easier for the novice player.

March in D Major, BWV Appendix 122

The charm of this march lies in the rhythmic vitality that results from the metric accent in the left hand and that of the syncopation in the right hand. Crisp *staccato* eighth notes in both hands in mm. 8 and 21 will evoke a trumpet sound accompanied by a military drum. Because of the quick tempo and the intricate coordination between the two hands, I would favor using the same finger on the left-hand repeated notes in those measures.

Menuet in C Minor, BWV Appendix 121

Beautiful ascending lines and an abundance of chromaticism make this minuet one of the more interesting and original of the entire group. It is possible to divide the opening ascending phrase into antecedent sub-phrases, which can be articulated with a slight emphasis on the second beat.

mm. 1-4

Similarly, it is possible to group mm. 17-22 into three two-measure phrases, each one departing from a slightly higher dynamic level. The final phrase (mm. 23-24) effectively releases the tension built up by the chromaticism of the three previous phrases.

mm. 17-24

Menuet in D Minor, BWV Appendix 132

The supple, sinuous right-hand melody blends perfectly with the angular left-hand lines, which often move in contrary motion to the melody. The B section, with its broad leaps of a tenth signaling a character change from seriousness to optimism and light, should be executed with a generous, well-balanced sound.

Menuet in G Major, BWV Appendix 116

The repetition of the two-measure motive in the beginning of the piece suggests the use of terraced dynamics. At the same time, the octave leap in mm. 2 and 4 imply an agile dancing gesture that is best achieved using a light *staccato* touch. The B section provides wonderful opportunities for fine dynamic shading, with its shift to different registers and its inventive harmonic scheme.

Polonaise in G Minor, BWV Appendix 125

The two opening unison phrases and the double notes in the ensuing measures suggest an imposing piece full of regal grandeur. The excerpt below suggests possible articulations.

mm. 1-4

In the repeat of the initial motive (mm. 9-10), the opposing motion of the leaps between the third beat and the preceding eighth note is a splendid surprise, worth highlighting with a strong expressive accent on the third beat.

mm. 9-10

An inventive approach to the left-hand articulation will add life and interest to the sequential character of mm. 17-19.

Polonaise in G Minor, BWV Appendix 123

The bold character of the initial right-hand statement features the typical Polonaise rhythmic motive. It returns in the left hand in mm. 9-10 and may be enhanced by using a *staccato-legato* articulation.

mm. 1-2

In contrast, the same rhythmic figure in mm. 3 and 7 sounds more natural played *legato*.

m. 3

The parenthetical fingerings in mm. 16-17 ensure a very smooth *legato* between the two voices in the right hand. For the left-hand line in mm. 15-16, the articulation shown below will provide a great deal of rhythmic interest and stability, suggestive of a stringed instrument, such as a *viola da gamba*.

mm. 15-17

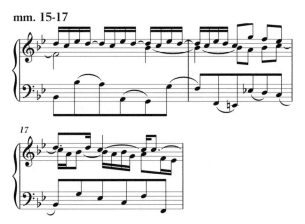

—*Christos Tsitsaros*

References

Carl Philipp Emanuel Bach. *Essay on the True Art of Playing Keyboard Instruments* (New York: W.W. Norton & Company, Inc. 1949, edited and translated by William J. Mitchell)

J.S. Bach. *Notebook for Wilhelm Friedemann Bach* (1720) *Neue Ausgabe Sämtlicher Werke* (Wolfgang Plath-Br).

Howard Ferguson. *Keyboard Interpretation from the 14th to the 19th Century* (New York and London: Oxford University Press, 1975)

Karl Geiringer. *Johann Sebastian Bach. The Culmination of an Era* (New York: Oxford University Press, 1966)

Table of Suggested Tempo Ranges

Title	Suggested M.M. Range
Polonaise in G Minor, BWV Appendix 119	♩ = 66-76
Menuet in G Major, BWV Appendix 114	♩ = 104-120
Menuet in G Minor, BWV Appendix 115	♩ = 80-96
March in G Major, Appendix BWV 124	♩ = 44-54
Musette in D Major, BWV Appendix 126	♩ = 69-80
Menuet in A Minor, BWV Appendix 120	♩ = 84-96
March in D Major, BWV Appendix 122	♩ = 63-72
Menuet in C Minor, BWV Appendix 121	♩ = 76-96
Menuet in D Minor, BWV Appendix 132	♩ = 104-112
Menuet in G Major, BWV Appendix 116	♩ = 108-120
Polonaise in G Minor, BWV Appendix 125	♩ = 60-72
Polonaise in G Minor, BWV Appendix 123	♩ = 60-72

Polonaise in G Minor

Composer unknown
BWV Appendix 119

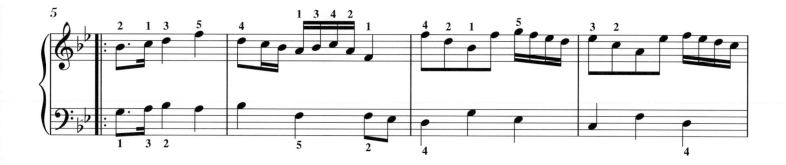

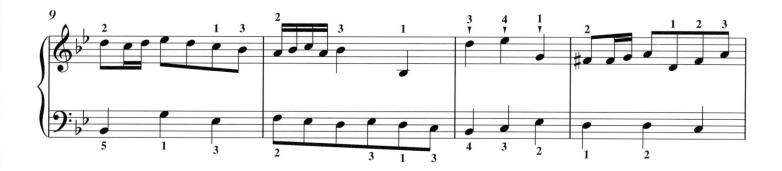

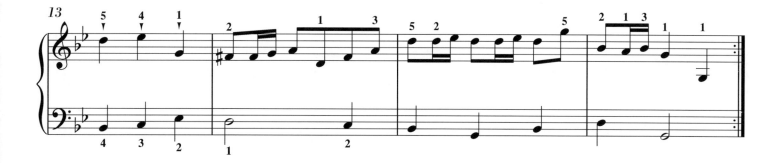

Menuet in G Major

Christian Petzold
BWV Appendix 114

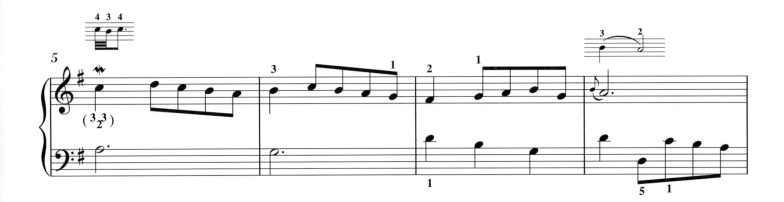

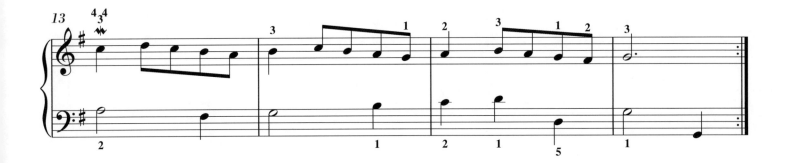

13

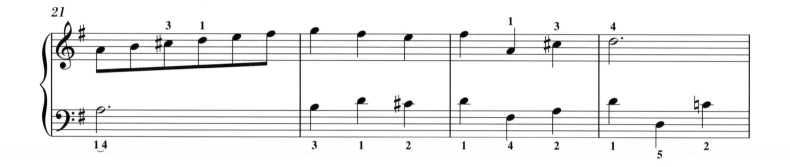

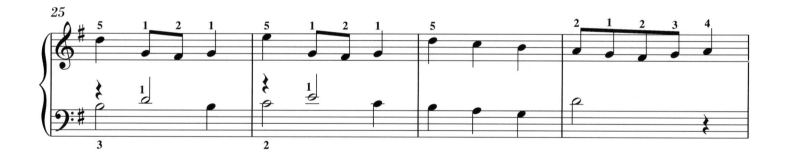

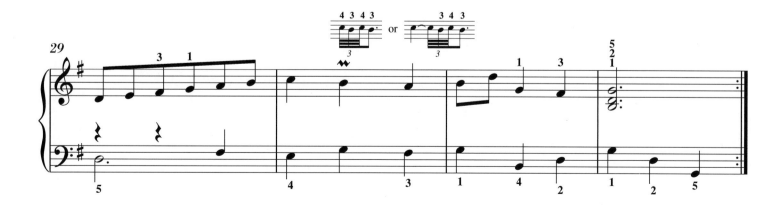

Menuet in G Minor

Christian Petzold
BWV Appendix 115

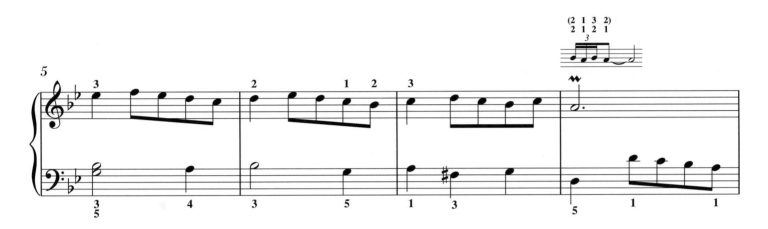

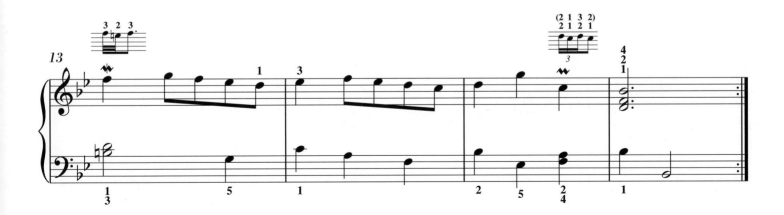

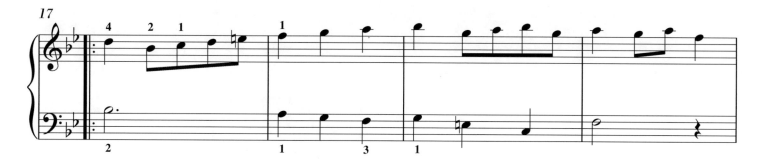

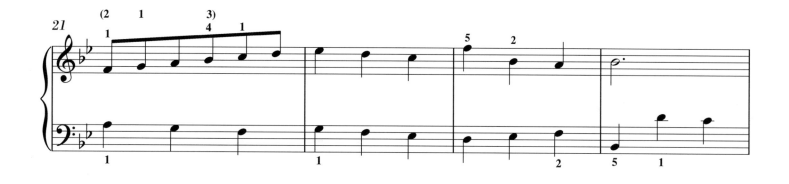

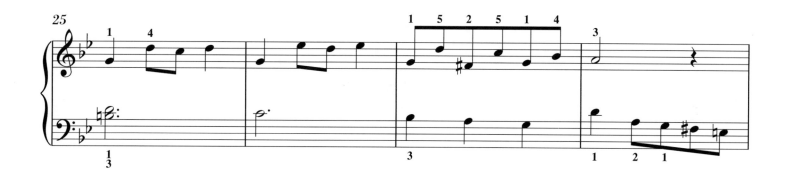

March in G Major

C.P.E. Bach
BWV Appendix 124

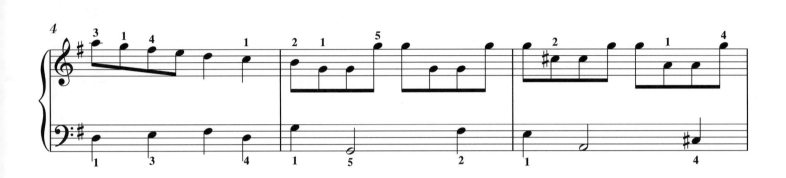

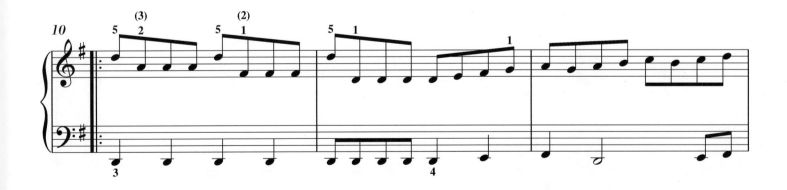

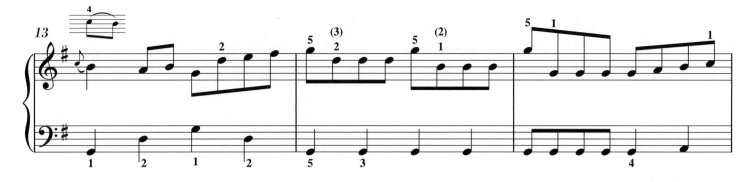

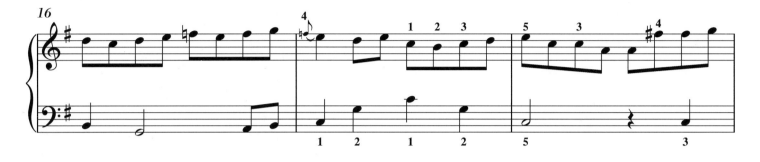

Musette in D Major

Composer unknown
BWV Appendix 126

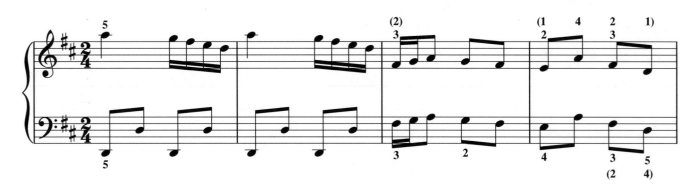

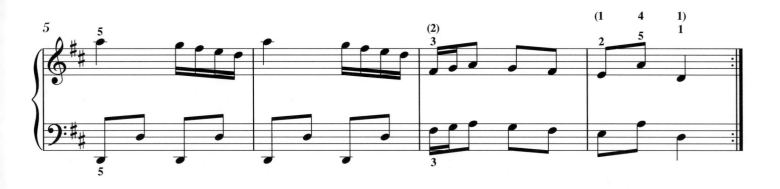

Menuet in A Minor

Composer unknown
BWV Appendix 120

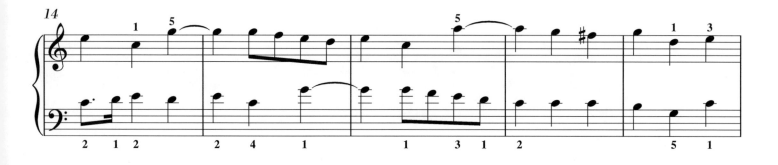

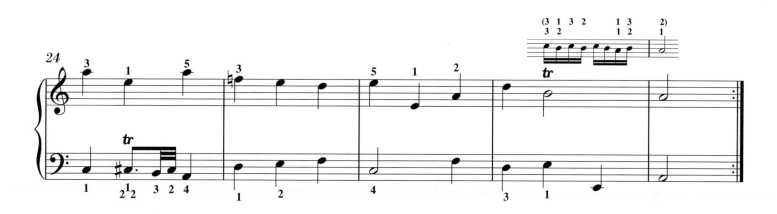

March in D Major

C.P.E. Bach
BWV Appendix 122

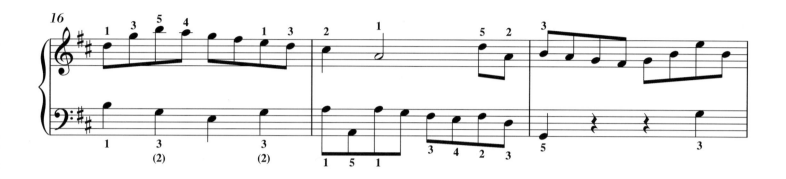

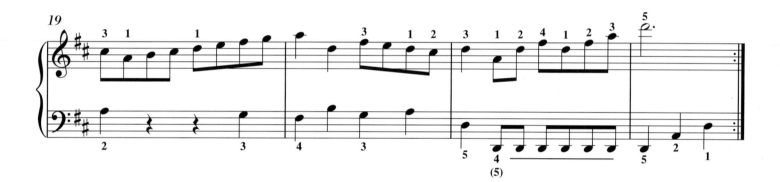

Menuet in C Minor

Composer unknown
BWV Appendix 121

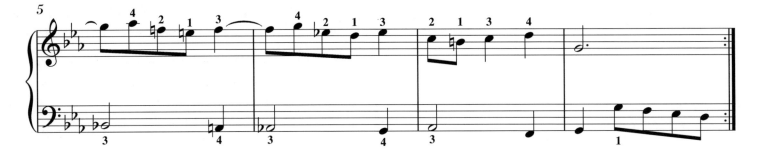

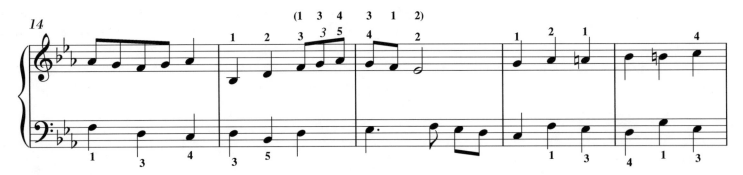

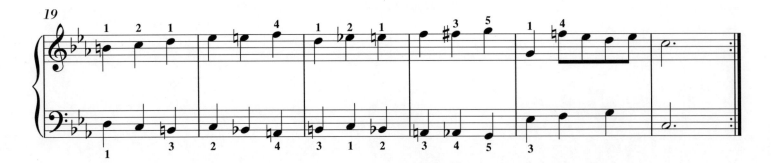

Menuet in D Minor

Composer unknown
BWV Appendix 132

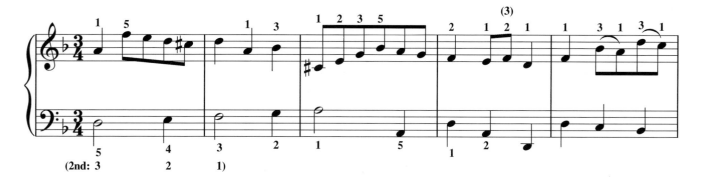

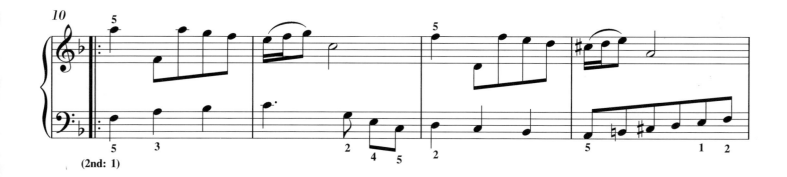

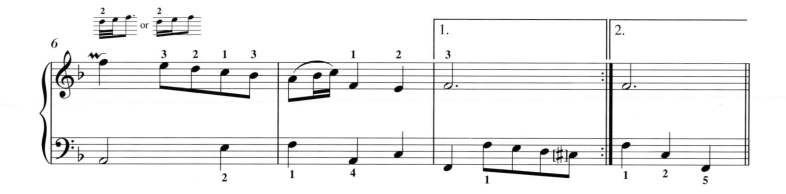

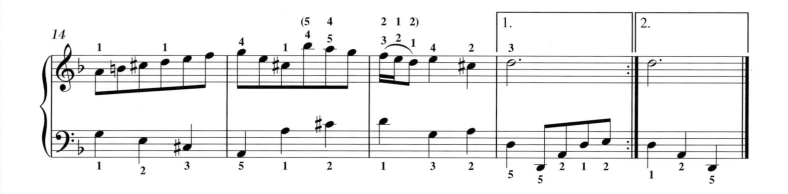

Menuet in G Major

Composer unknown
BWV Appendix 116

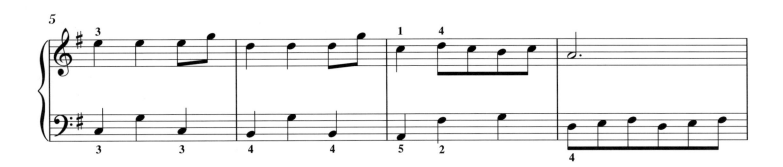

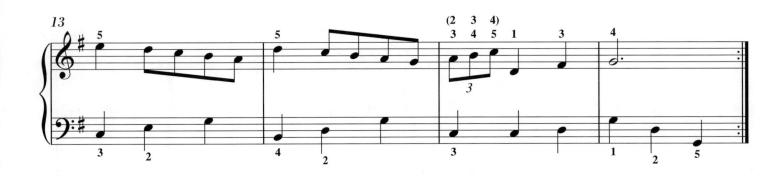

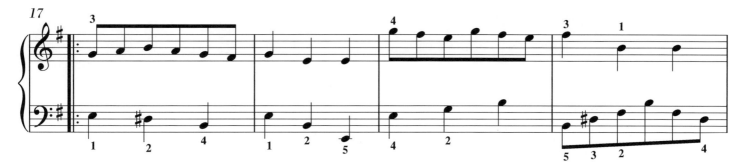

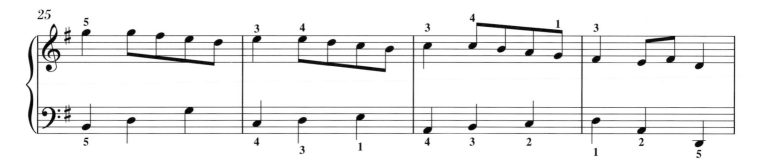

Polonaise in G Minor

C.P.E. Bach
BWV Appendix 125

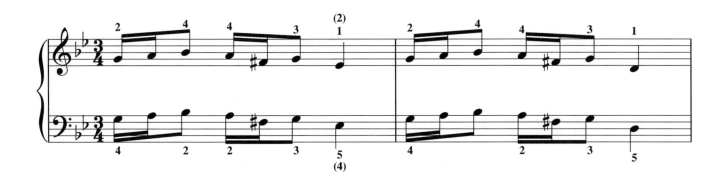

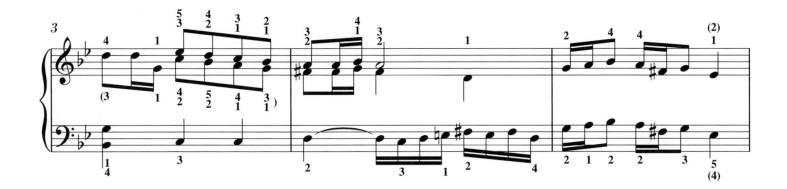

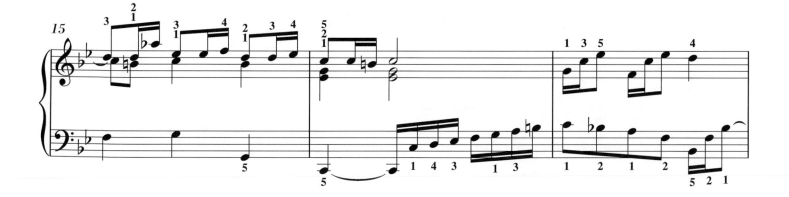

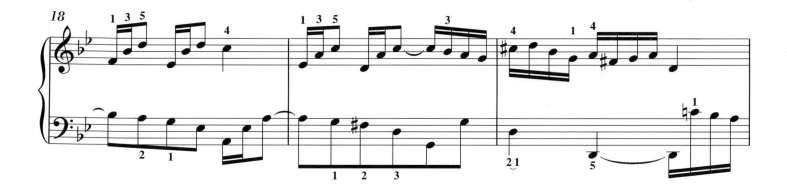

Polonaise in G Minor

C.P.E. Bach
BWV Appendix 123

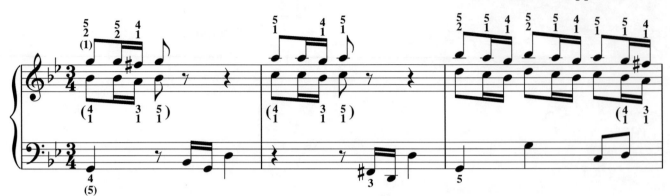

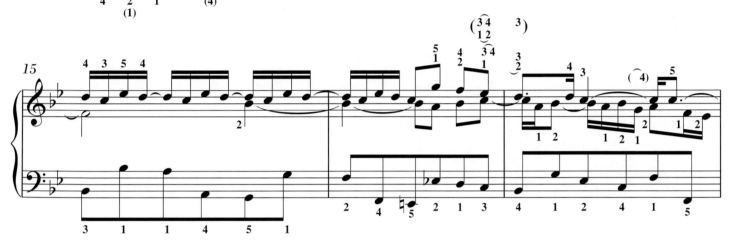

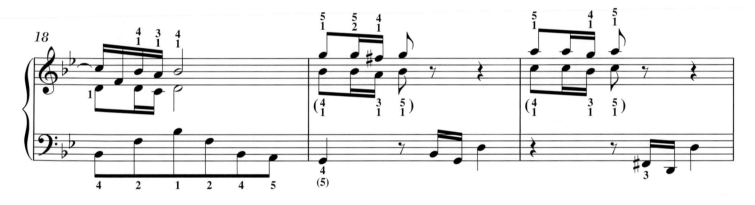

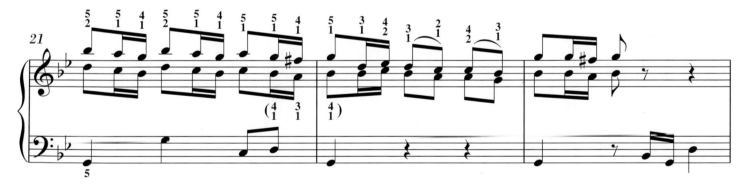

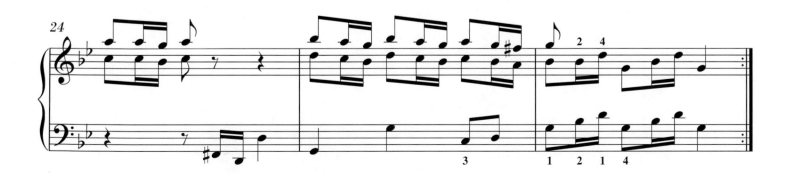

ABOUT THE EDITOR

CHRISTOS TSITSAROS

Christos Tsitsaros, contributing composer and arranger for the *Hal Leonard Student Piano Library*, is Associate Professor of Piano Pedagogy at the University of Illinois. He was born in Nicosia, Cyprus, and received his first formal instruction at the Greek Academy of Music. At the age of 13, he won first prize in the National Competition of the Conservatory of Athens. In 1979, he moved to Poland where he studied at the Frederic Chopin Academy in Warsaw under the guidance of Prof. Jan Ekier. As a result of winning the Gina Bachauer Institution Competition in Athens (1981), he continued his musical studies in Paris and graduated from the *Ecole Normale de Musique de Paris* within a year, obtaining the *Diplôme Superieur d'Execution* with distinction. While in Paris, he studied with pianists Aldo Ciccolini and Jean-Claude Pennetier. In 1986, a scholarship from the A. G. Leventis Foundation enabled him to study with Gyorgy Sebok at the School of Music of Indiana University in Bloomington, Indiana. There he received an Artist Diploma and a Master of Music degree (1989), and subsequently entered the School of Music of the University of Illinois where he attained a Doctor of Musical Arts in Piano Performance (1993). Soon after, he joined the faculty of the Piano Pedagogy division of the University of Illinois at Urbana-Champaign. Dr. Tsitsaros is also quite active as a composer, having won the composition competition of the National Conference On Piano Pedagogy, which launched an ongoing relationship with Hal Leonard Corporation. In 1998, Centaur Records released his first compact-disc album containing selections of his original piano works, and in 2001, he was artist-in-residence at the Helene Wurlitzer Foundation in New Mexico. He has participated in various workshops and conferences as a performer and lecturer, and has appeared as soloist, recitalist, and chamber musician in Europe and the United States. He gave his New York debut recital at Weill Carnegie Hall in 2001.